We Are Not These Hands

by Sheila Callaghan

A SAMUEL FRENCH ACTING EDITION

NEW YORK HOLLYWOOD LONDON TORONTO

SAMUELFRENCH.COM

Copyright © 2009 by Sheila Callaghan

ALL RIGHTS RESERVED

CAUTION: Professionals and amateurs are hereby warned that *WE ARE NOT THESE HANDS* is subject to a Licensing Fee. It is fully protected under the copyright laws of the United States of America, the British Commonwealth, including Canada, and all other countries of the Copyright Union. All rights, including professional, amateur, motion picture, recitation, lecturing, public reading, radio broadcasting, television and the rights of translation into foreign languages are strictly reserved. In its present form the play is dedicated to the reading public only.

The amateur live stage performance rights to *WE ARE NOT THESE HANDS* are controlled exclusively by Samuel French, Inc., and licensing arrangements and performance licenses must be secured well in advance of presentation. PLEASE NOTE that amateur Licensing Fees are set upon application in accordance with your producing circumstances. When applying for a licensing quotation and a performance license please give us the number of performances intended, dates of production, your seating capacity and admission fee. Licensing Fees are payable one week before the opening performance of the play to Samuel French, Inc., at 45 W. 25th Street, New York, NY 10010.

Licensing Fee of the required amount must be paid whether the play is presented for charity or gain and whether or not admission is charged.

Stock licensing fees quoted upon application to Samuel French, Inc.

For all other rights than those stipulated above, apply to: The Gersh Agency, 41 Madison Avenue, New York, NY 10010 Attn: Seth Glewen.

Particular emphasis is laid on the question of amateur or professional readings, permission and terms for which must be secured in writing from Samuel French, Inc.

Copying from this book in whole or in part is strictly forbidden by law, and the right of performance is not transferable.

Whenever the play is produced the following notice must appear on all programs, printing and advertising for the play: "Produced by special arrangement with Samuel French, Inc."

Due authorship credit must be given on all programs, printing and advertising for the play.

ISBN 978-0-573-69669-5   Printed in U.S.A.   #29078

No one shall commit or authorize any act or omission by which the copyright of, or the right to copyright, this play may be impaired.

No one shall make any changes in this play for the purpose of production.

Publication of this play does not imply availability for performance. Both amateurs and professionals considering a production are strongly advised in their own interests to apply to Samuel French, Inc., for written permission before starting rehearsals, advertising, or booking a theatre.

No part of this book may be reproduced, stored in a retrieval system, or transmitted in any form, by any means, now known or yet to be invented, including mechanical, electronic, photocopying, recording, videotaping, or otherwise, without the prior written permission of the publisher.

MUSIC NOTE

Licensees are solely responsible for obtaining formal written permission from copyright owners to use copyrighted music in the performance of this play and are strongly cautioned to do so. If no such permission is obtained by the licensee, then the licensee must use only original music that the licensee owns and controls. Licensees are solely responsible and liable for all music clearances and shall indemnify the copyright owners of the play and their licensing agent, Samuel French, Inc., against any costs, expenses, losses and liabilities arising from the use of music by licensees.

IMPORTANT BILLING AND CREDIT REQUIREMENTS

All producers of *WE ARE NOT THESE HANDS* must give credit to the Author of the Play in all programs distributed in connection with performances of the Play, and in all instances in which the title of the Play appears for the purposes of advertising, publicizing or otherwise exploiting the Play and/or a production. The name of the Author *must* appear on a separate line on which no other name appears, immediately following the title and *must* appear in size of type not less than fifty percent of the size of the title type.

PRODUCTION HISTORY

Commissioned by Eye of the Storm Theatre, Minneapolis, MN, 2002.

Developed by Soho Rep, 2004.

Workshopped by PlayPenn, 2005.

Produced by Crowded Fire with support from The Playwrights Foundation, 2006.

Produced by Catalyst Theatre, 2007.

CHARACTERS

BELLY – Young woman, early teens (15 years), tough, hard, street-smart, incredibly dirty

MOTH – Young woman, early teens (15 years), bright, sweet, a little bit manipulative

LEATHER – Man, age 35-45, manic and odd

AUTHOR'S NOTE

Punctuation is used to indicate delivery. Where no punctuation is indicated, delivery may be determined by the actor or director.

A stroke (/) marks the point of interruption in overlapping dialogue. When the stroke is not immediately followed by text, the next line should occur on the last syllable of the word before the slash – not an overlap but a concise interruption.

NOTE FOR ACTORS

While Belly and Moth's language seems infantile and they are described as young-looking, it is important not to have them come off like children, and their language should not sound like baby-talk. They are street-kids; cagey, jaded, and under-educated. The delivery of their language should reflect this.

Although Leather's language is halting, his delivery should not be. His speech is rhythmic, so it should not come off as a stutter but rather a rolling river of words with rocks here and there.

SPECIAL THANKS

Linsay Firman, Paul Meshejian, Larry Loebell, Michi Barrall, Maria Dizzia, Flora Diaz, Michael Dixon, Brent Popolizio, Travis York, T. Ryder Smith, Casey Stangl, Michelle Pett, Daniel Aukin, Frank X, Erin Weaver, Rainy Lacy, Maggie Chestovich, Summer Hagen, Paul DeCordova, The Jerome Foundation, The Playwright's Center, Kip Fagan, the MacDowell Colony, Julia Pearlstein, Sarah Fay, Shirley Serotsky, Scott Fortier, Regina Aquino, Casie Platt, Catalyst Theatre, Cassie Beck, Juliet Tanner, Paul Lancour, Crowded Fire Theatre, Ken Nicholson, the Düsseldorfer Schauspielhaus, Daniel Fish, Ronald Marx, Dagmar Domrös, Birgit Lengers, German Theatre Aboard, Lisa Joyce, Suzy Jane Hunt, Michael Rudko, Sarah Hart and Jay Jennings.

*(**SETTING**: Three spaces: one in the center of the room with six outdated computer screens and keyboards assembled haphazardly, power cords tangled and desks lopsided and mismatched, lights blinking. Each screen will display the titles of the scenes and various bits of text and scattered images throughout the play.)*

(The images should include [but not be limited to] the following, in random order: pornography, video games, breasts, celebrities, brand names, electronics, sex toys, corporate logos, weather, clothing, tooth decay, chat rooms, Flash animations, vacation destinations, muscled abs, etc. They may be displayed in a frantic feedback loop, or as static images, or both.)

(The text should appear as though it is being typed in real time, letter by letter, and should be presented as simply as possible to indicate a computer and a document.)

(The second space surrounds the knot of computer screens. It is sooty and bleak: dead trees with blackened trunks, wicker carts with broken wheels, cinderblocks, various bits of ripped cloth and garbage on a dirt road. Several shoddy, hand-painted wooden signs are stuck in the ground and point to the computers. They read "INTERNET.")

(The third space is located to one side, away from the computers and off the road. It has a crappy dresser and several rickety bunk beds.)

(The set should not be static, as the feeling of change should be present throughout the play. It should feel as though it is moving, or changing.)

One: The Lies Behind Your Eyes

*(**BELLY** is sitting by herself staring at the computers. She is sucking on an old grey banana peel very slowly. She is incredibly dirty, and has no shoes. She is also missing a few teeth.)*

(Text on the screens: "According to my research, a sustained economic growth of eight to ten per cent is anticipated over the next two decades. (!!) This province's market has surged ahead so quickly, experts say, by converting much of its economy to an 'unfettered' and 'possibly faulty version' of capitalism (CITATION NEEDED). The theory of the")

*(After a few moments, **MOTH** runs in. She also dirty, but less so than **BELLY**. Her hands are covered in black soot. She catches her breath, then approaches **BELLY**.)*

MOTH. *(a greeting)* Scuzzer...

BELLY. Scuzzer...

MOTH. Scuzzer-lover...

(They do some sort of elaborate handshake.)

What Angelfoot doin' today?

BELLY. Got the bang bang goin...

MOTH. BANG BANG!

BELLY. TWO gun-girls today...big black boots up to here, little camel shorts...

(They watch.)

MOTH. Cavity got the titties up?

BELLY. Yeah.

MOTH. Who he got?

BELLY. Bowleg. She onna bed now.

MOTH. Lookit them titties! How she walk?

BELLY. She not. Jes' lie there, rubbin'.... A'fore you come she kneelin' onna table with a hooey in her whatchit.

MOTH. Mercy...

(They watch.)

BELLY. Rutpig got hisself a new lady-talk….

MOTH. Yeah? How far he get?

BELLY. One leg movin'…other start soon….

MOTH. Where Booger? Booger never late…

(BELLY points.)

Oh. Hate when they switch machines. He too far away now.

BELLY. S'pose…

(A beat. MOTH is bored. She does something to amuse herself. It doesn't work. She is despondent.)

MOTH. Things sure isn't the same since the school blowed up.

(a beat)

BELLY. Wanner know what I think? I think they knowed it would blow up… Otherwised, why they had us making firecrackers in the lunchroom?

MOTH. Scuzzers.

BELLY. Anus-eaters.

MOTH. Coochie-flappers.

BELLY. CAPITALISTS.

(MOTH smells her hands and shudders. BELLY examines MOTH's dirty hands.)

You gotter drug 'em in the road til it come off. I drug and drug and it come off.

MOTH. Lookit! Rutpig other leg shakin…

BELLY. He gone for it…

MOTH. Go Rutpig…go rutpig…

(They both begin chanting "go rutpig" for a few moments, shaking their legs, until the inevitable happens. They react. Then…)

BELLY. Let's get inside, Mothie! Could get us a man talk. Jes' for fun.

MOTH. We got no coins, Bell. Asides, why they gone let TWO crazy kinkers in?

BELLY. Could try...we not try....jes' sit out here, watchin'...

MOTH. You seen Cavity. He walk like water. He don't got the wild-angry peepers like us. He half-lidded, like he seen it all. Even Rut pig half-lidded.

BELLY. I can be half-lidded

MOTH. Different for girls. Need more than half-lids. Gotter wear the sex-clothes.

BELLY. How you know about the sex-clothes

MOTH. My Mummer got the sex-clothes. From back when she work the Cooch club. Cavity always lookin' at the sex-clothes. Angelfoot with the bang-bang, all his gun-girls got the sex clothes

BELLY. The gun-girls isn't REAL, Moth, they is made up of tiny dots of colored light

MOTH. But still...lookit what covers the little dot-titties

(They peer into the café.)

BELLY. Huh. I got the sex clothes. Mine got fancy glitter-bits sewed in. Mine got little lights that spin around. My boots is REAL. Made of real skin. An' my camel shorts is MINE, not my old Momma's.

MOTH. Where you got it

BELLY. Prezzies. From Ma and Loopy and Crumbs and Dust. Send stuff every week. Big blue boxes with skinny gold ribbons and a million stamps.

*(Beat. **MOTH** knows she's lying but does not say anything.)*

*(**BELLY** knows that **MOTH** knows.)*

*(**BELLY** grows morose. She watches the café. **MOTH** watches **BELLY**.)*

MOTH. Something go down at Maidenhouse last night?

BELLY. No.

MOTH. You get slapped up by one a' the bigger girls?

BELLY. No.

MOTH. Needle try to take your tooth powder again?

BELLY. Nobody done nothing at Maidenhouse.

MOTH. Someone talk rank about your Pa bein' a Capitalist?

(a beat)

BELLY. *(quietly)* Yeah.

(a beat)

MOTH. They all scuzzers anywhat....

BELLY. He weren't no Capitalist!

MOTH. I know...

(A beat. **BELLY** *sucks on her banana peel, sulking.)*

BELLY. You wanner know somethin'?

MOTH. Yeah

BELLY. When I were four. I were a sentinel. I standed at the end of Big Road and I weared black boots that shined like they was wet and I carried around a machete strapped to my hip in a brown leather holder and I weared a bright red piece of silk wrapped around my forehead. I were seven feet high then. And I were a mens. And when kids run up to me I never smacked 'em, specially when they was crying and covered in white ash from when the school blowed up.

MOTH. I know, Belly.

(A beat. They watch the café. They notice something, then in unison they begin fake-picking their noses and chanting "go booger, go booger" until the inevitable wipe happens.)

(a beat)

BELLY. *(cont.)* Let's try tonight.

MOTH. But what if one of us get throwed out?

BELLY. The other throw herself out.

MOTH. I not know, Bell...

BELLY. Come on....

(MOTH *hesitates. Quietly,* BELLY *begins to chant "go Mothie, go Mothie..." Finally,* MOTH *smiles.*)

MOTH. Okay.

BELLY. Raaaah! Okay we need a plan. First gotter get the sex-clothes...

MOTH. Okay...

BELLY. THEN, figger how we git onna machine with no coins....

MOTH. Right.

BELLY. THEN, figger how we fine a man-talk to take us over.

(a beat)

MOTH. Over where?

(a beat)

BELLY. Nowhere.

MOTH. I thought the man-talk was for fun.

BELLY. Yeah. Yeah.

(An uncomfortable beat. They finish their bananas.)

Flasher got her earlobe cutted off. Came at her with the machete. SHING! Blood everywhere.

MOTH. Why?

BELLY. Prolly flappin' her cooch around. You know how she do. Flappin' that cooch around like a wet tuna.

(She demonstrates, making wet-tuna sounds.)

MOTH. What happened to the earlobe?

BELLY. Dunno. Found her on the lawn lookin' for it in the dead grass.

MOTH. Scuzzers.

(They continue to watch inside the café. Suddenly, **BELLY** *gasps.* **LEATHER** *enters.)*

BELLY. Lookit!

MOTH. New guy.

BELLY. Pretty clean-lookin.

MOTH. Leather bag…lookit all them coins he put in!

BELLY. Where he got so many?

MOTH. Maybe he stealed.

BELLY. No way he stealed. Get his hand chopped off. Got my hand chopped off 'cause I stealed a banana from Kicker when I were nine. Came at me with the machete. SHING! Blood everywhere. It growed back.

MOTH. Hands doesn't get growed back.

BELLY. Do.

(They watch.)

He a REAL mens.

MOTH. Mummer tell me go for the mens. Boys get you babies, mens get you homes.

BELLY. What we call him?

MOTH. Leather.

BELLY. Leather.

MOTH. Leather got a bunch of PAPERS with him…

BELLY. Leather gonna use him PAPERS in the CAFÉ

(They giggle and watch, continuing to hold hands. Then they begin chanting "go Leather, go Leather" and mimicking him adjusting his papers.)

(Text on the screens: "The theory of expansion, according to said experts, is not based on any grandiose economic premise, but on one simple idea: giving the ruling force the courage to let its people make money on ideas – which will eventually be turned into tangible goods and thus stimulate a thriving economy. (note: I HAVE NO IDEA WHAT THIS MEANS)")

Two: Not To Say He Isn't a Door

(LEATHER appears in another space. He is clean-looking and weary. He clutches a leather bag and speaks into a hand-held tape recorder.)

(The insides of his ears are black.)

LEATHER. It isn't it isn't it isn't. Okay. Just, and the noise, the the bling bling bling bling bling bling bling bling bling bling and me sitting there as though work were actually something that could, that that could be DONE. That I could DO. But. And and the PEOPLE, and the PORN, porn everywhere. So highly illegal. But then I, then so is the café I'm I imagine. But. You know THREE people threw up on the bus to the cafe tonight? Bad shocks, or. Or maybe the appalling diets of the, which would explain the the teeth, but. So they just leaned over and spewed right there, right in the aisle. Forty minute bus ride, Mother. And people SMOKING ON THE BUS. I mean I just. And the police here have KNIVES. HUGE ones. And they're EVERYWHERE, which makes no, I mean this is a time of peace, right? And people spit here, they spit everywhere, hawk and spit. On floors. I mean floors of BUILDINGS, Mother. Hhuh.

And my hostel? Shutters on the windows that don't even LATCH. And no mirrors, like ANYWHERE. And and of course no heat, and I asked the boy for extra blankets and he he just.

(Banging from outside. LEATHER covers the microphone of the recorder.)

ONE. SECOND. PLEASE.

(Banging stops. Back to the recorder.)

Sorry, I'm in the, I'm in one of those, one of those. Things. Anyway. Yeah. So. Ahhh. Forget it. Oh the bathrooms, or I don't suppose you can even CALL them, tst, there's no bath. And toilets? No. A TROUGH, Mother. With these little cinderblock walls that come up to your knees and a trough that you STRADDLE, okay, you squat over, over the trough in a straddle and let it, let whatever, dangle from you until you, and, and NO toilet paper, and of course if someone is squatting in the stall next to you they can just watch your stuff float by beneath them, and you PRAY that the bucket next to you is filled with enough water to wash it away. Because if it isn't. Well. I mean I mean. How much could pluming actually cost? What is this whole, okay preserving antiquity is swell and all but DO PEOPLE REALLY NEED TO SEE MY POOP?

(Banging again from outside.)

LEATHER. *(cont.)* You know. Working here isn't. Easy. Eating here isn't easy. Nothing. Not that I thought it would be, but. Again. No negativity. Because, because the sun is shining and the, I haven't been robbed and I'm I don't have dysentery, so. I think. I think I'm gonna cry.

(He shuts off his recorder and begins to cry. After a moment he pulls himself together and takes a deep breath.)

(He rewinds the tape and begins again. His demeanor shifts dramatically. He is hyper-cheery.)

So, alright, and HELLO and by the way, things are MUCH better today. Oh I'm in the broom closet of the opera house across the street from my hostel and so you might hear some, some banging occasionally because I think someone REALLY needs a broom. Heh.

So anyway. I found this stuff, this kind of resiny kind of sticky waxy stuff that comes in packages, like these sticks wrapped in plastic, and so that stuff I'm not sure what it's for but it's but I've been sticking it in my ears to block the noise at night and it's been working like a dream. Although it's heck to try and get it off my fingers. But what, right like this is a FASHION SHOW, or. Heh heh. NO. That's what, remember? When I'd get all dandied up for school, shoes spotless and those little striped ties, and you'd roll your eyes and say, "Darling, this is NOT a fashion show." Heh. Well mother, I've uh come quite a, quite a long way.

(He notices a spot on his shoe. He licks his thumb and wipes his shoe, oblivious.)

LEATHER. *(cont.)* But anyway. My work at the café today? Pages and pages of stuff. This is big, mother. It's going to be. BIG. No more abject poverty, ha-ha. No more ignominy, no more begging. All those snot-nosed little brothers of yours will be asking ME for chump change. And I'll LAUGH IN THEIR FACES just like they did to me. Ha-ha.

(He squints at his papers in the dim light.)

No light…and of course a lot of it is, it seems to be, huh, difficult to read…my hand cramps up so fast, then I've got like a, like a CLAW HAND, and then I'm trying to write stuff out and it's like OW, and uh of course they wouldn't yeah, have anything as efficient as a pr, a WORKING PRINTER at the, at the. So. Anyway. I'm about to, to recite my findings onto the tape, Mother, so if you aren't interested in my research then I suggest you fast forward. Okay. I'm about to start. Okay. Ready? And. Fast forward…NOW.

(He struggles to decipher his notes.)

Okay, date, 4 March, time, 23 hundred, and um, place, 24th meridian, heh heh. No. First item. Source: illegible. Uuummmmm. A. Compilation. Of. Of sources. Accompanied by my own insights. To be determined at a later. Um. So. Ba ba ba ba ba OH! Ahh, no, no, that's…gum. Um…..okay, here. Yada yada yada, god this isn't even MINE, where did…free ten minute foot massage?…. Okay. Okay. So. A society, an entire nnnnnnnnnation, at at…where's the rest…Ah Ha! And the question remains. The question….re…maaaaaaaaaains…

(He flips through his papers, lost.)

To be determined at a later date.

(He shoves his papers back into his briefcase.)

Okay, Mother Mother Mother Mother Mother Mother Mother Mother Mother Mother Mother Mother

Mother Mother Mother and I'm back. You, ah. Yeah. In case you bothered to sit through that. Turns out I didn't do as much, as much work as, as I'd. Huh. Well I suppose it's still. And I haven't even talked to any of the, the natives yet. Except the boy at the, and you know how that went. Oh and that prostitute. But that was just a blowjob, really. So.

Oh! You know. I. Had a. You were in a dream of mine this morning. No it wasn't a a dream really, it was a, a, a memory-type? Thing? I think we were in the old house. Anyway, you NEVER yelled, Mother, you weren't a yeller, but. This one morning you were yelling, at the maid. There was blood on the, a lot of blood, on your bed sheet. "What is this? Gracielle! What is this?" Remember? I was, I was confused because Gracielle had been with me all morning, she made waffles with whipped-cream faces but their mouths were straight lines and, and I asked "why aren't they smiling?" and she said "because they're bored." But, but so, anyway so you were yelling in the hall, and I I I said, "Mother, Gracielle was making waffles." And you. I think then you realized it was your blood. And you said. Quietly, you said. "Oh." And closed your bedroom door.

I was twelve I think? And I, and one day much later we were drinking cappuccinos in the sunroom and you, you told me I had lost a sister.

You know I never, um. Until this morning, I never connected the two, the two moments.

(a beat)

Okay. Signing off now. Misses and kisses, my beloved Mumster. Mooch mooch mooch.

(He pops the tape out, and pops another tape into the recorder. Presses play. A very old recording of a forties crooner-type begins to play.)

*(**LEATHER** listens a bit, and then he begins to dance.)*

(Banging is heard. He ignores it.)

Three: We Falter On the Verge of a Verge

(**BELLY** *and* **MOTH** *are outside the cafe. They are dressed part-clown, part-whore, part pop-star. Their make-up is wild and grotesque, and their hair is huge. They look completely awkward and uncomfortable,* **BELLY** *especially.*)

(*They check each other's make-up and steel themselves, then sneak inside the café.*)

(*Video games, techno music, rock and roll, modems connecting, spacebars clicking, keyboards typing, error bells dinging, and other shrill computer noises of our generation flood the air.*)

(*Leather is typing.*)

(*Text on the screens: "As one notable scholar (CITE!!) puts it, 'the psychology of desire transforms an idea into an asset.' The term 'psychology of desire' is particularly poignant to me at this moment, as I have immersed myself in said culture for an unspecified period of time and therefore I have witnessed an overwhelming _____. (note: COMPLETE THIS THOUGHT)"*)

(**LEATHER** *is reading from a computer screen. The insides of his ears are still blackened. A cup of coffee sits by his elbow.*)

(*He is typing furiously.*)

(*Slowly, and on tiptoe,* **BELLY** *and* **MOTH** *move into view behind* **LEATHER**. *They are attached to each other and their eyes are huge and wild, looking around.*)

(**LEATHER** *senses a presence behind him. He turns slowly, and sees the girls. He stares at them a moment, then turns back around and tries to continue working.*)

(**BELLY** *and* **MOTH** *begin moving their mouths weirdly, in a parody of seduction.* **LEATHER** *again senses them and turns around.*)

LEATHER. Good Lord. Okay. I, I I'm not sure what that, what that, what you're doing, there? With the. But it's clear that you want. Something. From me and. And although I have no doubt that, that you may think that is, um. EFFECTIVE, or uh uh COMMUNICATIVE, but. I have to, I just have to tell you that. Um. I am I'm at an utter, a a complete and utter loss.

MOTH. We seen you come in this morning. We peeper through the window. We peeper every day. Right Belly?

(BELLY is too terrified to talk. She simply stares wide-eyed and closes her mouth.)

LEATHER. Is she. Is she.

MOTH. She jes' hinkey. The lights and all. Bell? You hinkey?

BELLY. Unnnaaagggkk.

LEATHER. She doesn't look very. Um.

MOTH. She not ated since one banana last night.

LEATHER. Not what?

MOTH. Her tummy angry.

LEATHER. What? I don't under.

MOTH. Tummy angry. Need shiners. Bananas?

LEATHER. I have, uh, a half a sandwich?

(He reaches into his bag and pulls out a sandwich. He hands it to BELLY. She takes one tiny bite and then shoves the rest down the front of her pants.)

MOTH. She not always get feeded at Maidenhouse. The bigger girls take her stuff.

LEATHER. Yes, well. That was my dinner, so.

(BELLY digs into her pants to hand the sandwich back to LEATHER.)

No! No, it's it's. Keep it.

(BELLY shoves the sandwich back into her pants.)

(a beat)

LEATHER. *(cont.)* Well. If you don't mind. I'll just.

(He turns back around to do work. BELLY and MOTH remain behind him, staring. He senses them and turns around.)

LEATHER. *(cont.)* Truly, now. You want what, coins? Okay, I don't believe in, in begging. Okay because it does nothing for your economy if I'm, if I give you ladies money for for drugs or. Or candy or. Make-up or, or whatever it, it is. You. So.

MOTH. Are you a real mens?

LEATHER. What? Okay, parents? Do, do either of you have, any?

MOTH. I got a mummer and a Unkie. They home. Belly Ma tooked Crumbs 'cross the river when Belly were little. Loopy an' Dust already there. Her Pa supposed to bring her later a-cause she the youngest. But he. He didn't. Cause he got. Bell, what's that word, the big one?

BELLY. Tooked.

MOTH. No, the big one.

BELLY. Tooked. He got tooked away by mens in black shiny boots an' machetes strapped to their hips an' red silk around their foreheads.

MOTH. IMPRISONATED.

BELLY. *(quietly)* Yeah.

(A beat. LEATHER digs into his pocket and gives BELLY and MOTH two coins each. They stare at the coins in awe.)

LEATHER. Now, go. Play a. Look, someone just got up over there. Go on.

(BELLY runs off with the coins. MOTH hangs back, staring at LEATHER.)

(to himself) Unbe-unbelievable. With the, I'm like huh? Crisis, but I mean…. Hooo. Lu-GOO-brious.

MOTH. You talk funny.

(Startled, he whirls around.)

LEATHER. Ha! Mmmnnggg. I'm. Ahhhh. I'm not from around here.

MOTH. You from 'cross the river?

LEATHER. Yes.

*(**MOTH** is enraptured. She is silent for a bit, then the coffee mug catches her eye.)*

MOTH. Is that cafe? REAL cafe?

LEATHER. Coffee, yes. Bit watery, actually. And they don't have, they don't have cream. Or sugar.

*(**MOTH** stares at it, bug-eyed. He hands the cup to her. She takes it reverently.)*

(He notices her filthy hands.)

Goodness. Your hands.

MOTH. So?

LEATHER. What is it?

MOTH. Gunpowder. From packin' firecrackers.

LEATHER. It doesn't come off?

MOTH. You gotter drug your hands inna road. Belly drug and drug and hers come off. But I not drug. Like it. Remind me of stuff.

(She smells her hands.)

LEATHER. Soap, maybe?

MOTH. "Soap-maybe." "Goodness."

(She giggles.)

LEATHER. Pardon?

MOTH. Look like you kin use soap-maybe in your what-what's.

LEATHER. My what?

*(**MOTH** points to **LEATHER**'s ears. He begins wiping at them frantically.)*

Drat…No mirrors…thought I got it all…

*(**MOTH** continues to giggle.)*

Oh yeah, look at the old guy, with the with the dirty ears, ha ha…

*(**MOTH** laughs harder. **LEATHER** joins her in spite of himself.)*

LEATHER. *(cont.)* Oh yeah, isn't he just a a a fountain of fopishness, a a a monument of of misfortune…

MOTH. *(in hysterics)* A doody-eared dipshit!!

LEATHER. *(slightly less amused)* Yes, that too. D-don't spill…

(**MOTH** *nods, suddenly serious. She regards her coffee solemnly. She takes a long, luscious sip of it, eyes closed.*)

(**LEATHER** *watches her curiously.*)

LEATHER. You've. Never had coffee.

MOTH. No.

(She drinks again.)

LEATHER. You're very young, aren't you? I mean, you, you, you're very young.

MOTH. Not so many.

LEATHER. How, I mean, mind if I, how old…

MOTH. Ten plus five.

LEATHER. Goodness.

MOTH. What?

LEATHER. You seem so. Little?

MOTH. *(disappointed)* Oh.

LEATHER. I mean, that's not a, a bad thing, per se…

MOTH. What 'bout now?

(**MOTH** *begins to do that seductive thing with her lips.*)

LEATHER. Um, okay. Yes, you you look much older, now.

MOTH. Sex clothes help too. That's how we get inside.

LEATHER. What's the point of. If you have no coins. You can't DO anything, here. Can't get a machine, can't get a a a coffee.

MOTH. I know

LEATHER. So…?

(**MOTH** *shrugs.*)

MOTH. Jes'. Jes' wanner be inside.

(She closes her eyes and takes another deep, long, luscious sip of coffee.)

LEATHER. That's. Um. You can finish that.

(She does. **LEATHER** *watches her. At some point, she makes eye contact with him; a subtle, kind invitation. She hands him the coffee cup, then lifts her other hand and strokes his fingers.)*

Um. You. Have, have you ever, um. Had sex be, before?

MOTH. Yes.

LEATHER. Do, do you think you might. Want to? With me? I I mean, we don't HAVE to of course, I just, I thought, you know, with the, uh uh, although that might not be, huh.

MOTH. You wanner put your wonk in my tootie.

LEATHER. Um, y-yes. Among among other things.

MOTH. Now?

LEATHER. Well, not. I have a place.

MOTH. Okay. Lemme tell Belly.

LEATHER. *(relieved)* Excellent.

*(***MOTH*** looks around for* **BELLY** *but can't find her.)*

Where she go'ed?

LEATHER. Her coins probably ran out.

MOTH. *(knowing better)* Oh. Prolly.

*(***LEATHER*** gathers his papers anxiously, frantically. He is beaming.)*

LEATHER. Well. I just. Hoo. This is, this is. I didn't expect to come here today and find. I don't normally. But I said to myself, "Take a chance." Because one must, to to take chances in this life. And you, you seem so. So kind? There's not much, I haven't found. This place has not been kind to me. Yet. Until now. So. I thank you. I thank you for this. But I don't know um. Your. Your.

MOTH. Moth.

LEATHER. Moth. A little moth. Well. Shall we?

(He extends his arm. She doesn't know what to do with it. She extends hers as well. **LEATHER** *laughs out loud.)*

Very well.

(He takes her arm. They exit.)

Four: It Is Night That Makes Us Whole

*(In **LEATHER**'s hostel room. Three sets of bunk beds and a crappy dresser.)*

*(**LEATHER** enters with **MOTH**. **MOTH** immediately sits quietly on one of the beds.)*

LEATHER. Um so, welcome. Seems to be, empty now, last two nights there was a, HOOO, a backpacker-type with a STINK? My goodness, never smelled such a STINK. But he's gone. Ostensibly.

*(**LEATHER** retrieves a pack of cigarettes from a drawer.)*

Want one?

*(**MOTH** takes one. She pretends to smoke it.)*

Brought these over with me. I've noticed you can't get, um. You'd think cigarettes, for example, would be relatively easy to, to produce. Locally. But it doesn't. So. It's something I'm exploring in my work.

No no, you have to, um. Light it.

(He takes out a silver lighter and lights both their cigarettes. She takes pains to position it between her knuckles exactly as he has his. She places it to her lips repeatedly but does not inhale.)

(He removes his suitcase from beneath the bed, unlocks it, and retrieves a small plastic baggie from inside.)

You smoke? WEED?

*(**MOTH** shrugs.)*

Pot? Bud? Hashish? Ganja? Nick-nick? Farley-Drexel-Hatcher? I find it helps to. Helps to calm me. Because I tend to to to to be a little. You know. BBRRRRAAAANNNGGGG. Heheh. You look kinda. Are you, are you. Is this.

*(**MOTH** smiles.)*

Good. Because it's hard to. You know? Um. Music!

*(**LEATHER** retrieves his recorder and begins to play the 40's music from earlier. **MOTH**'s face lights up.)*

LEATHER. *(cont.)* Found it on the floor of the, the john actually. On the boat? It's. Yeaahhhh.

Um you know how um sometimes when you aren't, when you're you're lacking something huge but you can't quite say what, and you look down and…BAM. There it is. And it's EXACTLY what you need?

Kind of. Heh. Kinda like you.

*(**LEATHER** holds his hand out to **MOTH**. She takes it awkwardly, trying to maneuver the cigarette between them. They dance, very badly, for a few moments.)*

Do do do you have a boyfriend? Be-because I don't want some, you know. Big guy busts down my door middle of the, or your dad, or.

MOTH. No.

LEATHER. No. Okay. Lord. You are so. SWEET. You are so SWEET. I want to bite you.

(He leans into kiss her. She pulls back a tiny bit, thinking he is going to bite her. But then he kisses her, and she lets him. They kiss closed-mouthed, their lips pressed tightly against each other's, almost perfectly still.)

(A beat. They begin dancing again.)

Yes, yes, yes.

MOTH. These not my clothes/

LEATHER. My mother would FLIP over you. FLIP over you. She's. No longer alive, but. I still talk to her, I. Make tapes. All those tapes? Keeps me company. I don't know is that strange? I don't know it doesn't feel um strange, so. I'm. Hooo. I'm so tired? All of a sudden? Mother liked grapefruits and. And the woman at the desk. The woman at the desk? At the home? Mother was getting a little. So. Anyway. The woman at the desk had very long. Um fingernails. They curled like like corkscrews. She had trouble holding things, like. Pens, or. Mugs, or. And she couldn't type on a on a keyboard. Basically she answered phones. And pushed the food cart. Her fingernails…

MOTH. Like a she-devil?

LEATHER. EXACTLY like a she-devil. And they had scenes painted on them. Like. Um. Vacation scenes? Like beaches and palm trees, she. Spent a lot of money on them. Mother was, hah. Why am I telling you this? Mother was mesmerized. Couldn't take her eyes, off, off. Off the. The sunsets. But yeah, so. Grapefruit. Do you like grapefruit?

MOTH. No.

LEATHER. Oh, I do them nice. Cut out all the little triangles, then pour one dot of honey on each triangle. That way, you know, the flavor, is is even. I did this every morning. For mother. Because the woman at the desk? She couldn't. She COULD NOT. HOLD. A KNIFE. I'm so tired. Are you tired?

MOTH. No.

LEATHER. Ha. You must be so tired! I want to wipe that stuff off your face. Okay? Because it, it tastes very. Um bad. Okay? Can I do that?

(**MOTH** *nods.* **LEATHER** *grabs a towel and dips it into a jar of cream. He very gently wipes the make-up off her face.*)

MOTH. It cold.

LEATHER. *(not calm)* It's cold-cream, so. Ha! Actually never made the the connection. Until now. I'd like to take you to bed now. Is that okay?

MOTH. Yes.

(**LEATHER** *begins to undress.*)

LEATHER. *(not calmly at all)* Goodness. I could just talk and talk! I'm so calm. I've never met, um. Someone I feel so calm around. It's very…Encouraging? So.
Okay. Just a warning, I'll probably. My stamina is, isn't. What it should be, so. So basically I can't go very long the first four times. But after that I should be able to, to control things. So just, um. Yeah. Hang in there. Heh.

(**LEATHER** *has stripped down to his long underwear.*
MOTH *takes off her "boots."*)

LEATHER. *(cont.)* Do you, uh, need to get cleaned up, or. The hose-room is WAAAYYY down the hall. And the the water's probably frigid this time of. Of night.

(**MOTH** *shakes her head and stands shyly. She slides off her panties beneath her skirt and places them on the bed next to her.*)

LEATHER. *(cont.)* Okay. Um. Okay.

(**LEATHER** *moves toward* **MOTH** *and kisses her. He takes the cigarette from her and puts it out inside an empty coke can, along with his own.*)

(*He flips the lights off and sits on the bed. She sits next to him. After a moment, he slides his hand between her legs.* **MOTH** *takes a very deep breath.*)

MOTH. M-m-my Mummer when I done something not proper and she get real hotted-up at me know what she not call me Moth know what she call me she call me Black Death but you know when she not hotted-up at me when she lovey and her peepers is soft an' runny you know what she call me then she call me Goose Down but you know what none a' them my real name my real name done gotted lost when I were a bean bag an' no one can fine it not Mummer not Unkie not me not Belly but but…but…it okay…I think it okay…it okay…

(*She embraces him.*)

Five: Send Me There

(MOTH is sitting on the steps by the café, her elbows on her knees and her fists pressed into her cheeks to support her head. She is sound asleep.)

(BELLY appears.)

BELLY. MOTHIE!

(MOTH wakes up with a start and sees BELLY.)

BELLY.	**MOTH.**
Moth, mothie they throwed me out an' when I turn 'round to look you wasn't there, I thought they	I looked up an' didn't see you an' Cavity weren't there neither an' I was sure you was gettin' beated

BELLY. SCUZZER!

MOTH. CAPITALIST!!

BELLY. ANUS-EATER!

MOTH. COOCHIE-FLAPPER!!

(They sit down together on the steps.)

What happen to you? You there, you gone, I look around…

BELLY. Where YOU go'ed?

MOTH. You first.

BELLY. You seen me, right? I go'ed over to the machine…

MOTH. Yeah…

BELLY. I sit down an' look at the screen, and it SO BEAUTI-FUL, Mothie

MOTH. Yeah?

BELLY. Picture of a beach. Sand. Sun half onna water. Colors like orange an red an purple, in stripes. I stare dopey-like, an I think like if I keep on maybe I'll bust up inna million tiny dots of colored light an' then I'll be standin' there onna sand.

MOTH. Do you?

BELLY. Just WAIT. So I sticked my coins inna slot, like we seen all them do. And the beach, it TALK to me! It say, "you have thirty minutes." An' I say, "for what?" but the beach not tell me. So then I say, real loud-like, "THIRTY MINUTES FOR WHAT???" But it not say. So I make my slappers into two little balls an' I go BANG! BANG! BANG! onna top of the machine. Next thing I know, I'm movin' backward through the air with my shirt all tight an' bunched at my neck. Then I outside 'gain, an Cavity walkin' way from me like he a hero.

MOTH. Shirt-yanker.

BELLY. The worst! An' THEN, I a-member what we say 'bout if one of us gets throwed out first, so I wait. But you not come. I peeper back through the window, an YOU NOT THERE. An' I get so fraided, Mothie, an then I get breathey, you know, like I can't get nuff air into me, an' and my peepers is hobbin' and lights goin' grey and my freakies is numb an everything squeezin' down, squeezin' down…An I look down at my arms, Mothie, an' all I see is DOTS. Tiny dots. The color of skin. An' beneath my feets? Sand. And all around is stripes of colors, orange an red an purple. I INSIDE, Mothie!

MOTH. NO!!

BELLY. I THERE, inside it!!

But somethin' happen. And all a sudden I back outside the café looking up at the black sky. And then I puke.

(a beat)

MOTH. It all go away?

BELLY. Yeah.

MOTH. Why?

BELLY. I not know. Hinkey, huh?

MOTH. Yeah.

BELLY. Lets try 'gain tomorrow. Ask Rutpig to help maybe.

MOTH. He likely make us touch him wonk.

BELLY. Not care.

MOTH. You touch Rutpig wonk?

BELLY. Sure. S'Long as I go 'cross….

(**MOTH** *is quiet.*)

BELLY. *(cont.)* Mothie/

MOTH. Cross. Cross the river.

BELLY. Yeah. Touch a wonk, touch a whatsit. No matter. S'long as we gone. Right?

(*a beat*)

MOTH. Yeah.

(*a beat*)

BELLY. So…where you?

MOTH. Can't say.

BELLY. Why not?

MOTH. You get hotted-up at me.

BELLY. I not.

MOTH. Get all quiet and hurted.

BELLY. Why? It bad? You done dirt on me?

MOTH. No…

BELLY. TELL…I'll give you somethin'.

MOTH. What?

BELLY. Somethin' what I got.

MOTH. WHAT?

BELLY. Somethin' what you want.

(*a beat*)

MOTH. I. Go'ed off with Leather.

BELLY. Go'ed off?

MOTH. He stay at Snarler's mummer's ol' Guest House 'cross from Singin' Place. I go'ed with him.

BELLY. Why?

MOTH. He ask me to.

BELLY. Why he asked you?

MOTH. Maybe 'cause of the sex clothes?

BELLY. He put him wonk in your tootie?

MOTH. Yeah. He kinda goosey. Wear funny jammers, all long an' white. An' he talk an' talk, like he got the nerves. Tol' me 'bout his mummer.

BELLY. Where she?

MOTH. Dead. I think some lady with curly fingernails done dirt on her.

BELLY. A she-devil!

MOTH. Yeah. An' Belly, he have a Coca-cola can JES' SITTIN' OUT! Like it weren't nothin'. Bet he got a whole BOX a' Coca-cola somewhere.

BELLY. Bet he do!

MOTH. An' we smoke CIGARETTES?

BELLY. REAL cigarettes?

MOTH. Yeah. He light them with a shiny metal lighter with swirlies dug onna side. We smoke THREE EACH!

BELLY. *(squealing)* THREE EACH!! What else?

MOTH. Stuff. He. Put his. Kisser. On my tootie.

(a beat)

BELLY. What?

*(**MOTH** somehow demonstrates.)*

*(**BELLY** screams. **MOTH** screams. They both resolve into hysterics.)*

BELLY. *(cont.)* He NOT!

MOTH. Swear on my freakies, he done.

BELLY. Hol' up. Start 'gain.

MOTH. Well. First time it were jes' his wonk. That over soon as it start.

BELLY. Jes' like with the boys.

MOTH. Jes' like with the boys. But second time it longer, an he askin' "it okay? It okay?" An kissin' my face. Third time he. He do the thing first. With his kisser.

BELLY. What?

MOTH. Movin' round, I dunno. An' then he put his wonk in an' kissin' my face, "you so SWEET, you so SWEET" an' my head start goin' BOOM BOOM BOOM an' somethin' HAPPEN, Belly, my tummy get the wobble an' my noggin on fire an' my throat closin', an' something SPLODED!

BELLY. Sploded?

MOTH. YEAH. Like, like. Like the school done. I were so confused. An' I started with the boo-hoo. Couldn't stop. Bited my lip, bited my hand, but it jes' kept comin', boo-hoo-hoo. My boogers runnin', everything. An' he touchin' my hair, touchin' my face, like he my Mummer. "it okay…shhh…" an' kissin' me. An' then it stop. An' he hold me all tight-like.

(**BELLY** *is silent a long moment.*)

What you thinkin' Bell?

BELLY. Nothin'.

MOTH. Gone give me my whatchit now?

(**BELLY** *removes a half-eaten sandwich from her pants and hands it to* **MOTH** *silently.*)

What kine is it?

(**BELLY** *shrugs.*)

Do it got meat?

BELLY. I ated the meat. Got 'maters an' sauce an' other stuff.

MOTH. Thanks, Belly.

(**MOTH** *eats the sandwich.* **BELLY** *pouts a bit.*)

Taste good.

(**BELLY** *says nothing.*)

Bell…you said.

BELLY. Said what.

MOTH. You not get all quiet and hurted.

BELLY. I not.

MOTH. Lie.

BELLY. We not stuck together, is all.

MOTH. IS!

BELLY. I thought you got throwed out, or slashed up, or worsed. But you gettin' a tootie-tickle.

MOTH. He give you one too, Bell.

BELLY. I kin got my OWN tootie-tickle. An' not from some hinkey scuzzer.

MOTH. He NOT a hinkey scuzzer. He MENS. He from 'cross the river.

(a beat)

BELLY. Maybe he go back soon?

MOTH. Dunno.

BELLY. An' take us with him?

MOTH. Dunno.

BELLY. He not stay here forever…he got stuff there. Like. Work. An' people. An' he like you a lot.

MOTH. But that no reason to bring us…

BELLY. You think he make us pay? He no capitalist…

MOTH. Naw.

BELLY. We jes' get onna boat with him. An soon you see the beach I seen. And we THERE. An' I get to see Ma 'gain. Bet they gotta room for you too.

MOTH. A whole room?

BELLY. Yeah. An' after I fine ma, gone get one them glass boxes with the steam!

MOTH. What boxes?

BELLY. You know, glass box, lady with the wet hair an' eyes closed, steam comin' all around, then she sing an' the walls make her voice sound like apples…you seen that.

MOTH. No.

BELLY. Voice sound like apples fallin' froma tree. An' the box make you washed.

*(**MOTH** is quiet.)*

Mothie. Don't you WANNER go 'cross ?

MOTH. What if we can't got back?

BELLY. Maybe you not wanner got back. Maybe you love it there.

(a beat)

You gone see him 'gain?

MOTH. Tonight…

(a beat)

Wanner come?

BELLY. He give me the tootie-tickle?

MOTH. We kin ask him…

BELLY. Okay.

(a beat)

Know what? I peed in the mouth of a Capitalist once.

MOTH. Did he swallow?

BELLY. They always swallow.

MOTH. Figgers.

*(They giggle, but then **MOTH** becomes solemn.)*

Bell…If your own Ma not got you 'cross the river, how he gone?

(a beat)

BELLY. *(uncertain)* Because…Ma not from there.

MOTH. Oh.

(They both peer into the café.)

Six: You Take You Have You Want

(LEATHER is speaking into his recorder again. He is adorned in a bathrobe and slippers and has an ice pack pressed against his head.)

...this society is most, most. Brazenly? Bizarrely? Lodged between two worlds, past and present idealism and realism a nation nipping at the heels of of moderninity. Modernity. Modern. Ness. Billboards advertise foreign goods, but the economy cannot support them. One consequence of this is the, the sordid um rather addictive cyber culture that has infested um. Infected the nation. Internet cafes spring up illegally everywhere, and the natives? Natives...Citizens. Are drawn to them like. Like an ELECTRONIC OPIATE. Ooh, good. The, then the computer screens act as wa, windows into a glittering world of all the materialistic paraphernalia that, that they cannot. Buy. Afford? That they have no means to acquire. And the result of years and years of socialism. Is a. A quasi-capitalist, mostly antidemocratic, um. And so, the question remains. The question...re...mains...

(He flips through his papers.)

To be determined at a later, um. Date. Okay. Mother Mother Mother Mother Mother Mother Mother Mother Mother Mother Mother Mother Mother Mother Mother. Well, you'll you will be uh delighted to hear that I have not. Um, Vomitted? In the past several moments? I believe the the worst may have. Passed. Hooo. I am so tired?

(a beat)

She's. She looks very young, mother. She has, her neck is very thin. She has a very thin neck, and. Small breasts. And these immense wild eyes, and I. Ha, I wanted to bite her! She seemed, um. Frightened? At first? But I think she was. And she cried. A lot. You know, Mother, this, this is...I thought I heard her say the word 'love.'

At some point. I don't uh remember if uh, if she was saying it TO me, or or or just kind of SAYING, it, or. Or maybe I was the one who, who said it, but. At any rate.

(a beat)

LEATHER. *(cont.)* At least it's not, uh snowing.

(a beat)

Okay. I should. My head is, sheeew. I'm gonna make some tea. Oh, I bought this. The other day? This electric um, teapot-thing? And the woman? I asked the price and the woman just shook her head. So I asked again and she shook her head again. And so I said, rather loudly, "HOW MUCH DOES THIS COST?" And then she said, rather loudly, "HOW MUCH YOU WANNA PAY?" I mean, huh? So, so okay so I said, "um, three bucks." And she LAUGHED IN MY FACE. It's. Ha. You know? Nuts.

Anyway. Signing off now. Misses and kisses. Mooch mooch mooch.

(He shuts the tape off. He retrieves an electric teapot. He fills it with water and plugs it in.)

(A knock on the door.)

Um? Who is it?

MOTH. *(offstage)* Moth an' Belly.

(LEATHER *opens the door.* **MOTH** *and* **BELLY** *stand in the doorframe.)*

LEATHER. Goodness!
   (Re: **BELLY***)* I wasn't expecting, did we?

BELLY. We not see you today.

LEATHER. Oh, yes well. I've been a bit. Ill, I, I ate something, hooo. Bought it on a, on a stick, could have been anything. Goat, cow, rabbit.

BELLY. Rat.

MOTH. It usually rat.

LEATHER. Superb. I'm making some, some tea. Would either of you care for.

MOTH. Okay.

BELLY. Okay.

*(**BELLY** and **MOTH** enter somewhat awkwardly. **LEATHER** searches for some makeshift drinking cups and pours tea.)*

LEATHER. *(cont.)* So. What, uh. I mean.

BELLY. Moth say you from 'cross the river.

LEATHER. Um, yes, yes I.

BELLY. Why you here?

LEATHER. To, to study. I like to think of myself as a, a freelance scholar?

BELLY. You got a car?

LEATHER. Yes actually well no. I mean yes I had a car, several cars, two actually. One was a, a little ram-rod of a, of a. You know, four wheel drive and such? Don't suppose you know brand names….

(They stare at him blankly.)

No, well, it was a, a rather "fancy" one. It could. I guess this is excessive, but. Anyway it talked. Mine was a lady. I named her Lydia. LYDIA. It's so, um. Like a butterfly? And then my other car was a, a. A little red. Number.

(a beat)

Yeah, so, I sold both vehicles, so I could afford to. Um. Come here.

*(He hands them their tea. All three drink in unison. **BELLY** looks alarmed. She pulls a huge tea leaf from her mouth, disgusted. **LEATHER** does not notice.)*

LEATHER. *(cont.)* How how's the tea?

MOTH. Good.

BELLY. Good.

LEATHER. Good.

(a beat)

BELLY. Do you got people back there?

LEATHER. People. I have um COLLEAGUES, if that's what you, I have a COMMUNITY of SCHOLARS with whom I engage in SPIRITED DISCOURSE, so. So yes.

(a beat)

In the um lobby they have these flyers, with. Apparently there's a mountain. Do you hike?

MOTH. No.

BELLY. No.

(He looks at their bare feet.)

LEATHER. But you, you definitely can't. You need to bring your, I suppose sneakers will be f. With with good treads…

BELLY. When you gone back home?

LEATHER. Well, yes. Eventually I. Why?

BELLY. Because…

MOTH. Because…we…

LEATHER. *(agitated)* It's not like I'm in EXILE, or. Not like I was KICKED OUT or I could go back w-whenever I whenever people don't it's a FREE COUNTRY you understand so and I'm here for RESEARCH so. So any day I want, basically RESEARCH IS NOT ILLEGAL you know.

(He digs in his pocket and retrieves an inhaler. He takes a hit.)

(A beat. Calmly.)

(impressed with himself) I'm writing a book. I am DELVING, and. I can't really discuss it. I'm taking risks already, with the. There are no printers. Had to save it all on one machine. All the, my typed notes, uh et cetera. Gotta buy a disk, or. Anyway, it's a SECRET. Heh heh.

(He grabs his stack of his papers and tidies them conspicuously. Then he waves them around for the girls.)

These papers, ladies? They're all I need to become. A SENSATION.

(They look at him blankly. A beat.)

LEATHER. *(cont.)* I've been talking a lot. Why don't you. You girls. You talk.

*(**MOTH** and **BELLY** look at each other.)*

What, um. What did you do today?

MOTH. Rolled some balls made a' flour. Put 'em in a pan with oil.

(a beat)

LEATHER. Ah. And you?

BELLY. Fight in Maidenhouse today. Ratty pinched Peeler inna tit. Called her a fatass.

(a beat)

LEATHER. Ah. Well.

(a beat)

It gets dark here quite early. So.

MOTH. Belly an' me wanner ask you somethin'.

LEATHER. Of course.

MOTH. We wanner know if. If we kin go back with you.

LEATHER. Back. You mean HOME? What's, why?

MOTH. That where Belly family go.

LEATHER. Couldn't they send for her?

BELLY. They not know 'bout Pa. They still waiting fer me an' him to show up. But we not come.

LEATHER. Ah.

*(to **MOTH**)*

And what about, I mean *your* family is, is here.

*(A beat. **MOTH** lowers her eyes.)*

MOTH. *(quietly, shrugging)* Could come back an' visit. S'okay.

*(**LEATHER** is surprised and deeply touched.)*

Oh. You are. Ha. You must be the sweetest thing alive. I want to kiss you. Can I do that?

MOTH. Yes.

(LEATHER kisses MOTH sweetly and passionately. BELLY watches, becoming increasingly uncomfortable.)

LEATHER. *(cont.)* I'm so tired? I suppose heaving violently all afternoon can, ha, can take it's toll on on a man. So. I think I might like to go to bed now. It's been a truly delightful visit.

(to MOTH)

Would you. Moth, would you join me?

(MOTH hesitates, glancing back at BELLY.)

Oh. Well, if you don't. We can always, some other time...

MOTH. *(tentative)* Belly wanner ask you somethin' else.

(BELLY looks slightly ill.)

LEATHER. What?

MOTH. Go on, Bell.

BELLY. It nothin.

LEATHER. I'm um, I'm all ears, as they say.

BELLY. It nothin, Moth...

MOTH. Belly wanner know if you could / stick your

BELLY. NOT NOT NOT. It nothin'.

MOTH. *(surprised)* Bell...

(a beat)

LEATHER. Well now no need to be shy, or.

(BELLY and MOTH have a very expressive and intricate silent-eye conversation.)

Did something.

(BELLY and MOTH continue, adding small gestures.)

You know I don't quite know what to do when ladies fight.

(BELLY and MOTH come to a conclusion.)

(A long-ish beat.)

BELLY. *(quietly)* I missed my curfew.

LEATHER. Your.

MOTH. Maidenhouse gotta curfew. Sometime if she miss it she get beated.

LEATHER. What, someone HITS you?

BELLY. They doesn't like to get waked up. An' they doesn't got keys. Doors lock froma inside.

LEATHER. Oh. Well. There's beds, um. Here. I mean extra. They never, the girl at the desk never checks. So. Is that, I mean, is that…?

BELLY. Okay.

LEATHER. Well then. It will be like a. Ha! A Slumber Party, or. Uh.

(a beat)

And the hose room is down the.

(A beat. **LEATHER** *retrieves a toothbrush from his bag and begins to scrub his teeth.* **MOTH** *and* **BELLY** *watch him closely. He spits into an empty coke can. Then he strips down to his long johns.* **MOTH** *and* **BELLY** *stare at him as though they are waiting for something. They glance at each other.)*

LEATHER. *(cont.)* Blankets, extra blankets? No, okay. I have to leave pretty early in the. So.

(a beat)

Okay.

(He climbs into bed. **MOTH** *and* **BELLY** *choose beds to climb into, fully clothed.* **LEATHER** *climbs out of bed and turns out the light. Climbs back into bed.)*

(A long beat. **LEATHER** *sighs heavily.* **MOTH** *peers over her bed and stares at him. He peers over his bed and stares back at her.)*

BELLY. 'Night.

LEATHER. 'Night.

MOTH. 'Night.

(They all lay wide awake.)

Seven: To Run Is To Not Fall

(It is two days later.)

*(**BELLY** is sitting alone. She is staring into the café, anxious.)*

*(**MOTH** runs in, out of breath. She is disheveled and flushed.)*

BELLY. FINALLY! So? What he say?

MOTH. Got a lotta words. Jes' keep comin'. I nod, like this. I smile, like this. Sometime when he ask me, I rake his hair, like this. Rake, / rake

BELLY. What he SAY, Mothie?

MOTH. Lotsa stuff.

BELLY. Bout goin' CROSS.

MOTH. Oh.

BELLY. You ask him last night…

MOTH. Yeah…

BELLY. And…?

*(**LEATHER** scrambles in, clutching his briefcase, completely out of breath.)*

LEATHER. Well. Lovely morning. Good to see you again Belly, I haven't. It's been. What, a day?

(a beat)

You should come over for, for tea. Sometime. Because.

(a beat)

Good. Moth, you, you ran off, you're quite a. You run well.

MOTH. Belly were waiting.

LEATHER. Rabbit, or. Some small furry. Heh.

(a beat)

So. This is the back entrance. It's, ah. Dirty. Very dirty.

(a beat)

I'll just. Yeah. See you.

(He exits into the café.)

(The girls watch him through the window. After a moment, **MOTH** *smiles and waves inside.* **BELLY** *does not.)*

BELLY. You not ask him.

MOTH. I gonna.

BELLY. You PROM/ISED!

MOTH. I /know

BELLY. PROMISED!

MOTH. Gotter time it right!

(a long beat)

You not unner/stand…

BELLY. Not talkin' to you 'til you ask him.

MOTH. Bell…

*(***MOTH*** does a bunch of silly things [maybe only two] to get* **BELLY** *to talk.* **BELLY** *does not.)*

FINE! I'll ask him tonight.

BELLY. Spit swear.

(They spits into their palms and smack each other across the face, hard.)

Come back tomorrow early. So early it not even early.

MOTH. I will.

BELLY. I'll wait/ all night

MOTH. I WILL, Bell…

(They look inside the café. **BELLY** *glances at* **MOTH***.* **MOTH** *waves giddly into the café.* **LEATHER** *waves back. He types.)*

(Text on the screens: "Because it's all about choice, ultimately. The market depends on choice, as we all know, but too much choice imposed too quickly is ultimately destructive WHY??? EXPLAIN WHY!!!!")

Eight: It Is Day that Makes Us Frail

(**MOTH** *and* **LEATHER** *are in the hostel.* **MOTH** *is lying on* **LEATHER**'s *bed, beneath the covers.* **LEATHER** *has his papers spread across the floor, some in piles and some scattered randomly. He is sitting in the middle of the papers, scribbling furiously into a pad.*)

(**MOTH** *stirs in* **LEATHER**'s *bed.*)

(**BELLY** *is somewhere sleeping outside, waiting.*)

LEATHER. Why are you still in bed, little Moth? It's almost 11 am.

MOTH. Dunno.

LEATHER. You wanted me to wake you up early for nothing?

MOTH. Like layin' here. Pillow smell like you.

LEATHER. Well, little Moth, I am positively. On FIRE. Down here. Burning a hole right through the floor. Let me read you something.

(*He digs through his papers.*)

"I felt a presence behind me. I turned around – " No, wait. Present tense. Sorry.

(*He scribbles a bit.*)

Okay. "I feel a presence behind me. I turn around and see her. She has huge wild eyes and a long neck. And small breasts. She looks very young. Her huge wild eyes search mine, then the room, trying to absorb every commodifiable" – is that a word? – "commodifiable article in the room. She is" – baaa, something, I need a thesaurus. Um, where, okay ba ba ba ba ba oh. My favorite line. "In every gun blast, in every throbbing base line, in every augmented silicone bosom she sees her future, an unfurling ribbon of endless possibility. And what do I see in her? A people of innocence, hunger, and innocence." Hm.

And then I talk about the café, uhhhhh, I guess these are just notes. I'll read them. "Lax enforcement of fire codes. Neglect of authorities to regulate patronage. Overly restrictive licensing procedures." This is boring. Is this boring? "Metal bars on the windows. Water in puddles on the floor by knots of electrical equipment." This is boring. I'll stop.

(**MOTH** *smiling.*)

LEATHER. *(cont.)* You like it? It's sort of. I'm working from a, a new journalistic model. I mean initially I was going for, it was more of an economic academical sociopolitical intellectuary investigative-type whatever, but. But now I'm I'm layering in personal account to give it give it more of an. An emotional gravitas, so to speak? My goal is. Do, do you want to hear this?

MOTH. Yes.

LEATHER. Oh good. While not necessarily to make money, my goal is to to touch. As many people as I can. AND to make loads of money. Because this work is is is cutting edge! And people need to KNOW? They need to SEE that that the world does not revolve around their, their mp3 players and spa treatments and imported cheeses, and um. Whatevers. You know?

MOTH. Yeah.

LEATHER. But it's quite a task, because. See when something NEW is is, when folks are confronted with The NEW, can I touch you?

MOTH. Okay.

(**LEATHER** *begins stroking* **MOTH.**)

LEATHER. Okay, thanks. And to be perfectly honest, Moth, academia is. Restrictive? Folks saw me as an "eccentric," so. And my department? Well. And my dissertation? Well. And I suppose I would have stayed anyway, but. You know. She uh. Mother, she. But that's just the way things go, I suppose. Tea, do you want, or, I have a, a chewy from yesterday?

MOTH. Okay.

*(He hands **MOTH** a chewy from his pocket and plugs in the tea pot.)*

*(**MOTH** eats a tiny nibble of the chewy and tucks the rest away.)*

(Both her hands are completely clean.)

LEATHER. Mother had a bit of a, a following? Sang opera in her younger years. She was semi-famous, and, well, schools were kind to me, and. And she was generous with her fortunes, because. She had a lot. So. Cigarette?

MOTH. Okay.

*(He offers **MOTH** a smoke. She takes it.)*

*(**LEATHER** lights both cigarettes and inhales deeply.)*

LEATHER. Mother didn't understand my work, so. And then she lost her mind, so. And the money? Ha. Well. It's funny, actually. As she was dying? She she kept saying over and over. "I had a daughter once." This is boring. I'M BORING YOU. I'm such a.

MOTH. Keep talkin'.

LEATHER. Okay.

*(**LEATHER** prepares the tea.)*

Um so Mother's lawyer, you know, was in love with her. And he LOATHED me, he LOATHED me. I caught them kissing once. In the driveway? Saw them from my bedroom window. In front of his um, Saturn, or. But, but later that night? I asked Mother how the how the show was. "The tenor was too short, the soprano was too sharp, and Simon is a wretched kisser." Heh heh. FUCK YOU, SIMON…

*(**LEATHER** attempts to pour the tea. His hands are shaking noticeably.)*

So. Anyway, so when she told him to give all the, all her money to the fingernail woman. Simon said, "Okay." "Okay," he said. My hands are, ha! They won't stop shaking, isn't that funny? Um so so then he signed something, and then she signed something, and I think I need to be touching you when I say this, okay?

MOTH. Okay.

*(**LEATHER** abandons the tea and begins touching **MOTH**.)*

LEATHER. So w-we were all in her her little room with the bouquets and the the cards and the balloons, and the fingernail woman looked at the paper and fell down into a chair with her palms facing up and all her little sunsets twisting around and around and I I walked I walked slowly over to Mother in her bed and I grabbed the bar the the bar that that that kept her from rolling out and and I said I said calmly I said "Mother, you do not want to do this" and Mother said "I had a daughter once."

So.

So.

OH! I forgot, I completely….

*(He retrieves a medium-sized box wrapped in butcher paper from beneath his bed and hands it to **MOTH**.)*

I got it online. Had a little trouble, actually. My credit cards have been, uh. Shredded.

*(**MOTH** opens the box. It is a brand new pair of hiking boots. She holds them reverently, smelling them, rubbing them on her face, etc.)*

They, I ordered them from what-you-call-it. It's famous back home. They use that new high-tech, I got a pair for myself too. You won't get shin splints! And.

*(Delighted, **MOTH** puts her shoes on and stomps around. She then throws her arms around **LEATHER**, kissing him all over.)*

Well you're welcome, Little Moth.

MOTH. They heavy! Like I got two boxes on my feet.

LEATHER. Oh. I could send them back.

MOTH. No no no no no no…

*(She kisses **LEATHER** all over again.)*

LEATHER. Well. Well now.

(**MOTH** *grabs the tape player and searches through* **LEATHER***'s tapes. She retrieves the forties tape and puts it in.*)

LEATHER. What, what…Oh. C-careful, make sure it's the, the right.

(**MOTH** *begins dancing around in her new shoes.*)

LEATHER. Gosh. You are. SO. SWEET. And Wonderful? I uh, heh. Our hike will. I've never. I was always too, uh. And I had asthma as a child. But. And you know, I'll bet we get to the top? And we'll be laughing because, because I fell on the way up, or or something. That's cheesy, is that cheesy? I don't care! So I'll be covered in dirt, right, and and I'll throw you down and get YOU covered in dirt. And we'll be SO DIRTY? And our laughter will, like, echo around us. And. I'll take you there, Moth. Right there, in the dirt. I mean of course I'll have brought a,a blanket, so we won't have to, you know, be COMPLETELY in the dirt. But. But at any rate I'll take you. And when I'm done I'll take you again. And then I'll take you again. And it won't end, ever.

Let me, Moth? Let me take you forever?

MOTH. Okay.

LEATHER. Thank you.

(*a beat*)

Did, did you want your tea?

MOTH. Okay.

LEATHER. I bought this, it's flower tea? It's got little flowers floating in it. It was SO CHEAP. Everything is SO CHEAP! And the haggling, it used to stress me out, like WHAT DOES IT COST LADY, but, but now. I think I like it.

(*He hands her the tea.*)

Your hands are so clean.

MOTH. I drug them inna road. It come off.

LEATHER. Oh, and and you know what else is? I passed a market the other day, and they were selling chicken feet and and pig snouts, DEEP FRIED! TO EAT! People don't waste food here, it's. I COULD LIVE HERE. Buy a shack, or. I mean of course I want to finish my, my research before I make any like, permanent decisions, but. And I'm happy. I am happy! Let me build something for you. A chair, or. Do you need a chair? I don't know how to build one. WHATEVER! Ha ha! A ladder? That doesn't seem too hard. Are you happy?

(a beat)

Are, are you happy, Moth?

(A beat. **MOTH** *says nothing. She smiles wanly.)*

(uncertain) Good….

(He strokes her.)

(We see **BELLY** *outside the café, waiting. And waiting. She grows sleepy. She falls asleep.)*

(The next morning. **BELLY** *is still waiting for* **MOTH**. *And waiting. She grows frustrated. She grows panicky.)*

(Afternoon. **BELLY** *is still waiting. She pulls some coins from her pocket. She lays them out before her. She peers into the café. She gathers up her coins and tries to muster the courage to go into the café.)*

(She does. Something very theatrical and excellent happens here, as we see her explore the café euphorically.)

Nine: I Am Not One Knuckle, I Am a Fist

(**BELLY** *is sitting outside the café, drinking from a coffee cup.*)

(*Text on the screens: "DELETE PREVIOUS And so the question, for me, remains…how can the ruling force affect rapid economic and social change in said culture without disturbing the delicate balance of an unstable [thingie]? The answer, of course, is ffffff-gggggggbbbbbbbbb to be determined at a later IS RAPID CHANGE NEGATIVE IS WANTING MATERIAL GOODS BAD IS THE COST OF THE DISRUPTION WORTH THE RESULT ??????????????"*)

(**MOTH** *approaches, wearing her new boots. She is somber.*)

(**BELLY** *drinks her coffee silently.* **MOTH** *notices the cup. She is incredulous but says nothing.*)

(**BELLY** *notices* **MOTH**'s *new boots but also says nothing.*)

(*They sit in hurt silence for a long moment. Finally,* **BELLY** *speaks.*)

BELLY. Boots.

MOTH. Yeah.

BELLY. New.

MOTH. Yeah.

BELLY. Prezzie.

MOTH. Yeah.

BELLY. *(the ultimate insult)* Boot-girl.

(**MOTH** *is silent a moment. Beat.*)

MOTH. Where you got café? Someone come give it?

(**BELLY** *shakes her head "no" slowly.*)

(amazed) You get in?

(**BELLY** *shakes her head "yes" slowly.*)

How?

BELLY. Coins.

MOTH. Where you got coins from?

BELLY. Stealed from Leather. Had a hunnert bazillion inna drawer

MOTH. They wasn't YOURS, Belly!

BELLY. Those boots wasn't yours neither afore he give 'em to you.

MOTH. These was PREZZIES.

BELLY. I's acceptin' my prezzy afore it got gave to me.

(**BELLY** *continues to drink her coffee. Beat.*)

MOTH. What…what you do inside?

BELLY. *(shrugging)* Secret.

MOTH. What secret?

BELLY. Leather secret.

MOTH. What you mean?

BELLY. Tol' Rutpig, "Leather gotta SECRET on him machine. Help me fine it." Give him coins. He fine stuff. He read to me. Mos' stuff I not unnerstand. Stuff 'bout money. Bout polerticks. Bout you.

MOTH. What else?

BELLY. Leather gotter sell a book afore he go back. A-cause his book gone make him famous. And when he famous he get rich. An' he can't go back 'til he get rich an' he can't got rich 'til he get famous an' he can't got famous 'til he sell him book, an' he can't sell his book 'til he finish writin'.

(a beat)

Know how long he think it take him?

MOTH. Seven years.

BELLY. When he tell you this?

MOTH. Yestderday.

BELLY. What you say?

MOTH. Nothing.

(a beat)

MOTH *(cont.)* I sorry, Bell.

BELLY. Leave me 'lone.

>*(a beat)*

>*(***MOTH*** *digs in her pocket silently and hands* ***BELLY*** *a cigarette. She takes another for herself.)*

BELLY. Where you got these?

MOTH. Where you think?

BELLY. YOU stealed from Leather?

MOTH. Yeah.

BELLY. Thanks, Mothie.

>*(They put the cigarettes in their mouths, unlit. They pretend to smoke for a few moments.)*

MOTH. F-flasher find her earlobe?

BELLY. Flasher gone.

MOTH. What you mean gone?

BELLY. Some girls was in the hall doin' the boo-hoo. I say, "what the boo-hoo for?" They say, "Flasher dead. They kilded her." But I not think they kilded her. I figger somethin' worse.

>*(***MOTH*** *shudders. They pretend to smoke a few more moments. A beat.)*

>You know, after I ask Rutpig to fine Leather stuff…I ask him to fine Ma.

MOTH. Do he?

BELLY. No. But he fine other stuff. A pill make your wonk bigger. A baby giraffe inna jar. A potty shoots water in your bippy. A tree made a'glass. A machine brushes your teefs FOR you.

MOTH. Mercy.

BELLY. I see so much stuff I nearly splode. An' you know what Rutpig say? You can buy ALL of it if you got 'nuff coins. But you gotter know how to act. So I gone learn how to act. An' I gone fine Ma. An' I gone show up with a tree made a'glass a-cause I act right enough to got it. An I do it with or WITHOUT you.

(a beat)

MOTH. We'll think. Okay? We'll think real hard. We figger somethin'. 'Kay?

BELLY. 'kay.

(They fake-smoke and think. A long beat.)

Figger anything?

MOTH. No, you?

BELLY. Nah.

(They fake-smoke more. Long beat.)

BELLY. What about now?

MOTH. No, you?

BELLY. Nah.

(They fake-smoke more. Long beat.)

MOTH. *(re: cigarettes)* Bell, we doin' this wrong.

BELLY. How.

MOTH. We need fire.

BELLY. Fire make it burn up too fast. This way it last longer.

MOTH. Oh.

*(Another long beat. **BELLY** suddenly gasps.)*

BELLY. OH…

MOTH. What?

BELLY. OH…

MOTH. WHAT?

BELLY. *(very very agitated)* Oh oh oh…I got the IDEAR…

MOTH. What is it…

BELLY. It's BIG it's BIG…

MOTH. WHAT!!

BELLY. It's too big Mothie, I can't talk it…

MOTH. How m'I gone know what it is?

BELLY. I'll THINK it to you…

MOTH. Okay…

*(**BELLY** and **MOTH** grasp hands and squeeze their eyes down tightly. After a moment, **MOTH** gasps.)*

MOTH *(cont.)* OH…
BELLY. See…
MOTH. BELLY.
BELLY. It's BIG.
MOTH. It's THE WORST.
BELLY. I know.
MOTH. We CAN'T.
BELLY. I know.
MOTH. Ever.
BELLY. But what f'we not think anything else?
MOTH. We'll think somethin' else.
BELLY. There aren't nothing else.

(A beat. Both girls look a little ill. They look at one another. A decision passes between them.)

You a'member where they got the powder from?
MOTH. *(demonstrating)* Yeah.
BELLY. A'member what the boxes look like?
MOTH. *(demonstrating)* Yeah.
BELLY. A'member what the paper ties look like?
MOTH. *(demonstrating)* Yeah.
BELLY. A'member where the stringy bits go?
MOTH. *(demonstrating)* Yeah.
BELLY. A'member how the paper get folded?
MOTH. *(demonstrating)* Yeah.
BELLY. A'member where the glue come from?
MOTH. *(demonstrating)* Yeah.
BELLY. A'member the bowl of water nearby?
MOTH. *(demonstrating)* Yeah.
BELLY. A'member the other bowl of sand?
MOTH. *(demonstrating)* Yeah.
BELLY. A'member how to measure the grit in your hand, like a cup?
MOTH. *(demonstrating)* Between the big straight wrinkle an' the curved broke wrinkle.

BELLY. A'member the weight of the grit?

MOTH. *(demonstrating)* Like a pig foot.

BELLY. A'member how we roll a paper cone to drop the grit inna tube?

MOTH. *(demonstrating)* Spread the sand out beneath. Not wipe your eyes. Not breathe too close to the cone. Not talk while you pour.

BELLY. We measure everything double this time. We set testers off in the Pit.

MOTH. You think the Pit still there?

BELLY. What else they use it for?

MOTH. You think Storehouse still 'round?

BELLY. Folks still makin' firecrackers….

MOTH. You think they fine us when we done?

BELLY. No.

(a beat)

MOTH. You think. You think.

BELLY. Everything I think…you already know.

MOTH. But…what if he figger was us done it? Get all hotted up, go cross an' leave us behind…

BELLY. He not leave without you.

(MOTH says nothing.)

He not, Moth, would he?

MOTH. *(small)* I not know.

BELLY. Hinkey scuzzer…

MOTH. He NOT a hinkey scuzzer…

BELLY. F'he leave us behind he a / hinkey

MOTH. *(wildly)* Say 'gain I'll tear your gob off!

(BELLY is stunned. A beat.)

BELLY. *(quietly)* 'Kay.

(a beat)

MOTH. When we do it? Tomorrow?

BELLY. Tonight.

MOTH. Tonight.

*(**MOTH** begins to shake. She goes to smell her hands to calm herself down, then realizes they are already clean.)*

(The text on the screens: "there are considerations")

Ten: His Arms and Legs Replace Themselves

(**LEATHER** *talking into his tape recorder.* **MOTH** *is sitting the bed in the hostel. It is night.*)

(**MOTH** *is going through the motions of packing firecrackers with her hands.* **LEATHER** *does not see her.*)

Okay so yesterday I decided to go for a bike ride along the, the main road? And. And I rode pretty far out. Things got busier, traffic, whatnot. Cars, I haven't seen cars in a while. And. And there was a little, a store front? Not a stall, an actual, glass enclosed…It looked brand new. So I parked the bike and. I walked in. Music? Kind of cheerful and um. You know soft lighting? And clean? And and a counter, and a smiling fella in a baseball cap, "what can I getcha?" And above his head a bright orange menu and the um lettering all white and lowercase, and I ordered the first thing I saw. Grilled vegetable sandwich with goat cheese and sundried tomatoes on rosemary focaccia. And a cup of organic Guatemalan roast. And then I moved to the, the register? And I told the girl what I ordered? And I asked, "HOW MUCH DOES IT COST?" And she said, "EIGHT-FIFTY." And I took out my wallet and I gave her some bills and for a tiny second I wondered whose hand that was, giving her my money.

And. And so I got my tray and sat down and ate two-thirds of my sandwich and it was tasty but I was full so I threw the rest in the garbage, and. And then I drank my coffee. Six sugars. Four creams. My coffee was. It was. Perfect.

(a beat)

So. So the whole.

And in regards to myself. Or, I mean. My thesis. There are, um. Considerations.

(A beat. **LEATHER** *regards his hands.)*

Mother…

I don't understand the shape of my hands.

*(A long beat. **LEATHER** looks at **MOTH** uncomfortably. He places the recorder down and sits next to her on the bed.)*

LEATHER. *(cont.)* You're very quiet.

*(**MOTH** shrugs.)*

I mean you're usually quiet, but. Like listening-quiet. Now you're like thinking-quiet. What, what are you thinking?

*(**MOTH** shrugs.)*

Are you thinking about the sandwich shop?

*(**MOTH** nods.)*

I know it's…right? I'm exploring it in my, ah. Revision.

(a beat)

Moth. Tell me what's wrong.

*(**MOTH** holds out a box to **LEATHER**.)*

Why?

*(**MOTH** shrugs.)*

It's not my birthday, or…

*(**LEATHER** opens the box.)*

…ah…

(He pulls out a beautiful butt plug. He holds it up, wiggles it, explores it in various ways.)

MOTH. It was my Mummer's. She threw it out when I were a bean bag. I saved it.

*(**LEATHER** wipes his hand on his shirt, slightly horrified but not wanting to seem impolite.)*

LEATHER. Ah. Your, your. Your mother's. Do, do you know what this is?

MOTH. Somethin' for your bippy.

(She points to her butt.)

Ahh….

MOTH. I jes' think it's pretty. Mummer's favorite color.

LEATHER. Well thank you. I love it. I do. Hm. Drill a hole, put it on a chain, or?...Gosh you look so sad...

MOTH. M-my noggin.

LEATHER. Your

MOTH. My brain. Hurts.

LEATHER. Yes, mother got those at least twice a week. I used to rub her scalp. Would you like me to do that?

*(**MOTH** nods. **LEATHER** begins to rub her head.)*

There now. You'll be asleep in minutes. It always works.

*(**LEATHER** begins to fall asleep, rubbing **MOTH**'s head.)*

(drifting) ...you know I get the feeling your friend doesn't like me very much...she's like a...a big...

*(**LEATHER** is asleep. **MOTH** checks to make sure. Then she slides off the bed and kisses **LEATHER**'s head.)*

(She grabs his leather bag and yanks out his papers. Then she pops his tape out of the tape recorder and shoves it into her pocket. She exits.)

Eleven: I Wake To Dream

(Sound of fireworks. A very theatrical explosion happens.)

(Text on the screens: "Please insert coin for the next twenty minutes.")

*(**MOTH** and **BELLY** run screaming in. They are out of breath and their hands are covered in black.)*

(Smoke pours in.)

MOTH. Nobody were in there, right?

BELLY. My hands

MOTH. Nobody were in there, right Belly?

BELLY. My hands is on fire!

*(**BELLY** drags her hands in the road. **MOTH** begins breathing hard.)*

MOTH. He seen! That feller 'cross the road seen us!

BELLY. No one seen nothin'

MOTH. The smell…

BELLY. Smell like the school done…

MOTH. Why the whole thing go up? Why not jes' the one machine?

BELLY. Maybe we use too much…

MOTH. Belly the world shuttin' off, it squeezing down…

BELLY. Breathe hard.

MOTH. My freakies is numb!

BELLY. Breathe harder, Mothie…like you drownin'….

*(**BELLY** and **MOTH** cling to one another and breathe very hard, hyperventilating, their eyes closed. The sound and air around them changes, is darker, higher-pitched, tighter.)*

*(Slowly, **BELLY** and **MOTH** become fuzzy, as though their molecules are breaking apart.)*

(A sunset blooms around them steadily, and sand appears beneath them. All is grainy and pixelated, made up of dots of colored light.)

(**BELLY** *opens her eyes.*)

BELLY *(cont.)* Mothie…look….

(**MOTH** *looks around in wonder, then down at her dot arms.*)

MOTH. Everything is dots!

BELLY. Yeah…

MOTH. It a hallucernation?

BELLY. Yeah…

MOTH. It BEAUTIFUL…How long it last?

BELLY. Not so long…we prolly puke soon.

MOTH. Okay.

(*A beat. They are calm now, taking in the sunset.*)

BELLY. Can't believe we done it, Moth.

MOTH. Yeah…

BELLY. But I wish the whole thing not go up.

MOTH. *(cont.)* Where you think Rutpig'll go?

BELLY. Maybe he start writin' letters.

MOTH. An' Angelfoot?

BELLY. Join the military. Get a machete an' a piece a' red silk an' a gun.

MOTH. An' Booger?

BELLY. Professional Booger-picker.

MOTH. *(giggling)* An' Cavity?

BELLY. He grow his own titties so he not hafta leave him room…

(*They burst into laughter. After a moment.*)

I gone miss it.

MOTH. Me too.

(*a beat*)

We gotter get names now.

BELLY. We got names.

MOTH. Real names. People names.

BELLY. Why?

MOTH. A-cause. Things is different.

BELLY. Don't know too much names.

MOTH. Me neither.

BELLY. Maybe we get 'em onna boat.

MOTH. Yeah.

I not feel so good.

BELLY. Me neither….couple more seconds.

(They hang on to one another and watch the sunset.)

(After a moment, the shadows of two men holding machetes appears…or a siren is heard…at any rate something happens to suggest that the girls have been caught.)

(They react.)

(The computers disappear in a cloud of smoke.)

Twelve: It Is Not Valour, But It Has Its Own Light

(It is three weeks later.)

*(**LEATHER** is packing up his suitcase. He finishes, then sits on his bed looking weary and lost. He wears **MOTH**'s butt plug around his neck on a chain.)*

(Construction sounds outside.)

(He reaches for his tape recorder.)

LEATHER. So. I put in yet ANOTHER call to Uncle Auggie. His new wife seems to think it will, there will be no problem, I just show up whenever and she'll, um. So. And that cat of theirs died, so. Heart attack, they think. So my allergies won't, won't be so, um. Debilitating? One hopes.

I'm so tired? I've been making phone calls, so. Seems I should be okay for about three months. Financially, I mean. As long as I am. Conservative, and. And I've been speaking with some lawyers. Okay ONE, and yes, it's Simon. He said he'd "see what he can do." He actually sounded happy to hear from me. Said he was, ha, he was worried. RIGHT. But.

So. I'm just gonna. I have to tidy up a bit.

(a beat)

I dreamed about her again last night. She was. Yeah.

*(He turns off the tape recorder. He sits on his bed and reaches beneath. Pulls out a box. Opens it and removes a pair of hiking boots, identical to the ones he gave **MOTH**. He slides his feet into them and stares at them.)*

*(A knock. He opens the door. It is **MOTH**.)*

LEATHER. *(shocked)* H-hello.

MOTH. Hello.

LEATHER. Come in.

(She does.)

I thought I'd never, you, you. You've been. Away.

MOTH. I were sick.

LEATHER. Three weeks! I would have, uh. Taken care of you, or. You, you know that.

MOTH. I know.

LEATHER. So, so, why didn't you. I mean.

MOTH. I were fraided.

LEATHER. Of what?

MOTH. You'd be hotted up at what we done.

(a beat)

LEATHER. My papers?

(**MOTH** *nods.*)

The café?

(**MOTH** *nods.*)

Wow. I mean I might have GUESSED, but. That, that. I mean. You could have been killed.

MOTH. We wasn't/ even

LEATHER. And actually, this this whole time, and no word, I thought for sure, I mean I WENT there, you know I SAW what was left, which was NOTHING, few cinderblocks some puddles of melted plastic and the rest was just like, little black things floating in the in the air, and I kept I went everywhere, but I I didn't know where you, or your last name, or ANYTHING, checked THREE different hospitals, then I, I just I just SAT here, staring at the wall…waiting for you…but you but…

MOTH. You gone start yellin'?

LEATHER. No, no. I'm not a yeller. But I mean *CHRIST!!! YOU COULD HAVE DIED!!! OTHER PEOPLE COULD HAVE DIED!!!*

MOTH. We checked a-fore…

LEATHER. And why, okay, I mean the WHOLE PLACE?

MOTH. We jes' meant to do your machine…

LEATHER. And what if you had, had gotten CAUGHT??!! I mean I've HEARD things, they're, they're, I mean it might just be rumors, but. But, I mean.

MOTH. *(quietly)* We done.

(MOTH shows LEATHER her right hand. It is gone, replaced by a bandage.)

LEATHER. Oh. Oh Moth.

MOTH. It don't hurt. Mostly just itches. But I not think it gone get growed back.

(A beat. LEATHER is confused.)

LEATHER. Why?

MOTH. So you'd go home an'…an take me with you…

(LEATHER is deeply touched.)

LEATHER. No one's ever blown anything up for me before.

(A tender beat. LEATHER gestures to his suitcase.)

M-my boat leaves at six. Tonight…

(a beat)

They have. I mean, I've seen excellent, um. Prosthetics? Over there? You know, fake, um.

(He wiggles his hand.)

And my uncle is a doctor, he might know someone. I'm staying with him. Temporarily. He has a fairly large home and he's never there. I mean, what can he do if I, you know, I just freaking SHOW UP with you? I mean he's an asshole, but. He's got a good heart.

MOTH. An' Belly?

LEATHER. Oh. Well, she can. I mean, I suppose. Where, where is she?

(MOTH opens the door. BELLY is standing in the doorway, smiling shyly. Her right hand is also missing.)

BELLY. Hello.

LEATHER. Hello, Belly.

BELLY. That not my name no more.

LEATHER. Oh? What is it?

BELLY. Elloise Kittenbottom. But it gone change. Soon as I fine Ma.

LEATHER. How do you plan on finding her?

BELLY. I'll figger when I get there.

LEATHER. Oh. Well.

BELLY. Moth got a new name too…

LEATHER. You do?

(MOTH nods.)

Go on.

MOTH. Lydia.

LEATHER. *(smiling)* Lydia. Like a butterfy.

BELLY. You got a real people name?

LEATHER. I do. It's Phillip.

BELLY. What it mean?

LEATHER. I don't, uh. It was my grandfather's name.

BELLY. It hinkey. Sound like a thumb.

LEATHER. How exactly does, does something SOUND like a thumb.

BELLY. It jes' do.

LEATHER. Well, thank you Ms. Kittenbottom, but I am keeping it.

(a beat)

So. I don't suppose you, you both have much to pack…

BELLY. We brung bags…

*(**BELLY** whips out two small plastic bags with some clothes stuffed inside.)*

LEATHER. Ah. Well.

(An awkward beat.)

Oh. Moth, do you need to. Your family…

MOTH. I not tell them.

LEATHER. Don't you think you/ aught to

MOTH. No.

*(**BELLY** touches **MOTH**.)*

LEATHER. Oh. Alright.

(beat)

BELLY. What all the noise for?

LEATHER. The bathrooms. New plumbing. And up the street they're, um building something as well. Sandwich shop, or. Hey, if we wait around long enough we won't even have to go anywhere because everything will start making its way over TO US! Ha! Or. Huh. I guess it. It already has. Um.

*(**LEATHER** whips out a near-empty pack of cigarettes.)*

Last one. For now.

*(He lights it. Takes a drag. Hands it to **MOTH**. She smokes. Hands it to **BELLY**. She smokes. **BELLY** hands it back to him.)*

So…

(Banging is heard furiously outside, along with drilling and clanging and other construction sounds; the euphony of progress.)

*(**LEATHER** smokes deeply, calmly.)*

So.

End of Play

**Also by
Sheila Callaghan...**

Ayravana Flies, or A Pretty Dish

Crawl, Fade to White

Dead City

Scab

That Pretty Pretty; or, The Rape Play

Please visit our website **samuelfrench.com** for complete descriptions and licensing information.

From the Reviews of
WE ARE NOT THESE HANDS...

"Bold and engaging, *We Are Not These Hands* is as fun as it is engaging...Rich in detail and full of humor and pathos."
– *Oakland Tribune*

"Swaggering eccentricity...Callaghan takes a lavish mud bath in a broken language...Ripe apocalyptic slang; at its best, it's racy and unrefined, the kind of stuff you might imagine kids in the back alleys of a decaying world might sling around."
– *The Washington Post*

"The gap between rich and poor yawns so wide it aches in Sheila Callaghan's *We Are Not These Hands*, but much of the ache is from laughter. *Hands* is a comically engaging, subversively penetrating look at the human cost of unbridled capitalism on both sides of the river...the anger of the play's social vision is partly concealed by its copious humor, emerging more forcefully after it's over...*Hands* bristles with bright, comic originality, particularly in depicting the limitations of its people."
– *San Francisco Chronicle*

THE SCENE
Theresa Rebeck

Little Theatre / Drama / 2m, 2f / Interior Unit Set
A young social climber leads an actor into an extra-marital affair, from which he then creates a full-on downward spiral into alcoholism and bummery. His wife runs off with his best friend, his girlfriend leaves, and he's left with… nothing.

"Ms. Rebeck's dark-hued morality tale contains enough fresh insights into the cultural landscape to freshen what is essentially a classic boy-meets-bad-girl story."
- *New York Times*

"Rebeck's wickedly scathing observations about the sort of self-obsessed New Yorkers who pursue their own interests at the cost of their morality and loyalty."
- *New York Post*

"The Scene is utterly delightful in its comedic performances, and its slowly unraveling plot is thought-provoking and gut-wrenching."
- *Show Business Weekly*

TREASURE ISLAND
Ken Ludwig

All Groups / Adventure / 10m, 1f (doubling) / Areas
Based on the masterful adventure novel by Robert Louis Stevenson, *Treasure Island* is a stunning yarn of piracy on the tropical seas. It begins at an inn on the Devon coast of England in 1775 and quickly becomes an unforgettable tale of treachery and mayhem featuring a host of legendary swashbucklers including the dangerous Billy Bones (played unforgettably in the movies by Lionel Barrymore), the sinister two-timing Israel Hands, the brassy woman pirate Anne Bonney, and the hideous form of evil incarnate, Blind Pew. At the center of it all are Jim Hawkins, a 14-year-old boy who longs for adventure, and the infamous Long John Silver, who is a complex study of good and evil, perhaps the most famous hero-villain of all time. Silver is an unscrupulous buccaneer-rogue whose greedy quest for gold, coupled with his affection for Jim, cannot help but win the heart of every soul who has ever longed for romance, treasure and adventure.

SAMUELFRENCH.COM

THE OFFICE PLAYS
Two full length plays by Adam Bock

THE RECEPTIONIST
Comedy / 2m., 2f. Interior

At the start of a typical day in the Northeast Office, Beverly deals effortlessly with ringing phones and her colleague's romantic troubles. But the appearance of a charming rep from the Central Office disrupts the friendly routine. And as the true nature of the company's business becomes apparent, The Receptionist raises disquieting, provocative questions about the consequences of complicity with evil.

"...Mr. Bock's poisoned Post-it note of a play."
- *New York Times*

"Bock's intense initial focus on the routine goes to the heart of *The Receptionist's* pointed, painfully timely allegory... elliptical, provocative play..."
- *Time Out New York*

THE THUGS
Comedy / 2m, 6f / Interior

The Obie Award winning dark comedy about work, thunder and the mysterious things that are happening on the 9th floor of a big law firm. When a group of temps try to discover the secrets that lurk in the hidden crevices of their workplace, they realize they would rather believe in gossip and rumors than face dangerous realities.

"Bock starts you off giggling, but leaves you with a chill."
- *Time Out New York*

"... a delightfully paranoid little nightmare that is both more chillingly realistic and pointedly absurd than anything John Grisham ever dreamed up."
- *New York Times*

SAMUELFRENCH.COM

www.ingramcontent.com/pod-product-compliance
Lightning Source LLC
Chambersburg PA
CBHW070649300426
44111CB00013B/2333